Practising Ascending

Practising Ascending
© Nadine Hitchiner / Cathexis Northwest Press

No part of this book may be reproduced without written permission of the publisher or author, except in reviews and articles.

First Printing: 2023

ISBN: 978-1-952869-82-2

Cover Art by Sofie Kohaupt
Design, Editing & Layout by C. M. Tollefson
Cathexis Northwest Press

cathexisnorthwestpress.com

Practising Ascending

Poems
Nadine Hitchiner

Cathexis Northwest Press

For my husband

Table of Contents

Introduction

Prologue	1
On Poetry: Would We Call it Danger, or Odyssey?	2

Origin

Like the Men in My Family	11
I Dreamt I Visited My Mother in Her Garden	12
Sixteen Songs for the Catbird	13
Acknowledgement	15
Laissez-Faire	16
Counting Sheep	17

The Learned Lover

Poem with Lines from My Grandmother's Phone Call/Ekphrastic Poem after a Fantasy of a Man Dancing on Water	21
Ode to the Spit Sip	23
Kummer Aufsatz	24
Regrettably,	26
Piano Quai	27
Song for George	29
Esther	31
Engine Study in Oil	32
Within Origin	33
Conservatory	34
Dear George	35
Chronology Dice	36
Jukebox	38
Memo for the Reader	39

The Learned Crop

To the Carnivores in Spotted Treelight	43
Darius, I've Stopped Imagining Things	45
Memoir of a Twerk, Read to a Dark Room	47
Eye Training	49
Kummer Feld, Kummer Gericht	51
On Birds	52
The Coroner's Hairbrush	55
Hunting Season	56

Forgive the Window   57
Brushsmith   58
Tristan   60

The Learned Water

Portrait of His Love as a Widower   67
Eons   69
To The Streets of Hong Kong that Glisten with Their Sadness   70
Paperboy   71
Love in Particular   73
I Try Not to Place a Brow in   75
Review of an Ache   76
What Do You Expect Me to Say, Clearly I was Disappointed   77

The Re-Learner

Dear Youth, I Dream Tonight in Arms that are Gentle   81
Canoe   83
Self-Portrait as Tinder   84
The Other Woman   86
If I Could, the River   87
The Good Summer   88
Persephon, Persephone   89
Small Theories   91
Seagull Pantoum   92

The Learned Ascender

To Touch a Rose like an Abacus   97
My Loneliness as Kafka's Diaries   99
Fruit Basket   100
Portrait of a Spring as a Parody   101
Hourglass   102
Kiwi Science   103
Enough to Look   104
Love Poem as Oblivion   105
What Good   106

Introduction

Prologue

Matrjoschka

My maiden name is still on the postbox, the doorbell, and I've told my brother
all about the voices. In the fridge's conservatory, the carrots and milk—always a winter ahead.
We're never low on milk—if it came down to it, we could make our own snow, say each doubtful
season, *this is the light I come from, this is the light you come from. Let the others make angels or devils out of us.*
There'd be plenty of us. Give me this much doubt: if christianity is true, the first day is in its many
trillions—each morning, our light gets its evolution, and it'll do. In my cashew-soft fingers,
one of the handmade cups my brother gave us as a wedding gift; a ghost in *real gold*
(as he pointed out) brushed onto it. The house is still warm with scraps
of August that will soon fade as the year eats at it. I'd just squeezed the last of the plums
into the bin, given the laundry its second cycle of redundancy. The flowers—six vases
of hydrangeas, apple stalks and some blossoms that I cannot name, will remain
for almost three weeks before the eucalyptus starts to rot at the stems, and I will not
be bothered by it. For days now, I've been bringing apples to the trees. Asking. On good batteries
I've run for miles, all the way from January through mid-April. Came back and combed the hair
in the drains—asked, if I could pull my shit back out of the Altkleidercontainer and then, the thrift
stores; feels I haven't seen myself in years—the multiverses I remember;
I've been many kinds of people: the good, the bad
(predominantly bad at trying to be good). Now I'm just someone with a good imagination.
My father told me, he'd once gilded an apple—I thought of it, when my mother
gave me a Matrjoschka—I thought being a wife would do to me something
similar that other names have, but I'm still so utterly the same,
that it scares me to find it beautiful.

On Poetry: Would We Call it Danger, or Odyssey?

1. *Letter*
inspired by Gia Marie's sculpture plaster artwork on canvas, titled "New Beginnings"

At first, it was the moon that, without its vowels, was an alphabet. I wrote plenty when the sky was clouded, and light spread like a law. When there wasn't a pool in the garden. Now, in the heat of evenings, there is poor language in the water: "oo-h's" and "aa-h's", as the neighbours' bodies sink into it. A round offering, involuntary as a knee-jerk—it is its softness that I envy. I'm soft

in all the wrong spots. Do you think
it would rain frequently without the moon,
or am I just making up a myth? It stormed
earlier, the dog came back in. If I ached, until you ached, how

would we measure this kind of distance? Would we call it danger, or odyssey?

If we stared at a poem hard enough, long enough, would the elephant in the room forget why it returned? Would it still know how to mourn,

with all that technique?
I tell people, "I am a lovée in love", and you know what tongues are like; "la vie?—est belle!"

Wish I could give something back to the light of my lover—besides my shadow! I'd lay only my head on his shoulder, but egg-shaped as desire. Into the big dipper, playing pinball at Café Mix. That one time, he'd zip up, and come back with a sparrow (out for a smoke, standing by the back door). Bless him, he's as good at heart as he is at the hands, and sometimes his gifts are so unintentional!

All of my fifty-minute best friends ask, "where is your anger?" I meant to tell them this before: "I saw a sculpted scarf, called 'New Beginnings', and realised that even motion can become a statue." In my dream, I went into the neck of the woods and screamed—"aa-h! Aa-h!" Suddenly, I was the woman in the scarf of beginnings, and the woman was me, writing. Then, it was me who lost something, but seemed bigger than before.

2. *Motels in the Air*
to P.

My husband and I drove, middle of this year, to the house we lived in for eight seasons. The wind, although summer, like cold spasms in the air. And I observed: whatever wave rose and fell again—the water remained. I stood next to it—my creativity, osmosed. Had not cared about its body, either, its multi-aptitude and rooms—motels in the air. But your poem came from the time you hid, and likewise, from the time that was hiding from you—I made the bed in its room, before I left it, which means it, too, was water coming from water.

Each chamber, I filled differently, and it filled me differently. In the river-room, my consciousness was the river-room, and the doors and windows were open: I saw from it the room of rain and admired its gaps, the brief fall and recurrence of it.

At the house, he positioned the grill on the grass belt around the flowerbed, so it looked like the roses were smoking, and the smoke then gathered thick—I wanted to tell it, the way you'd dare tell a ghost—someone without innards, the mirrors had been smoking, too. My reflection: a mist, dry like a mother's handshake. Testing, attempting to imitate a cloud, to absorb what water it could find in the air, and extinguish where it came from;

last year, the year I most echoed its endurance, I shovelled twelve steps into the house—there was a blizzard; each flake, definite as time; had lung and blood. I drove through the streets anxious, bitter. Hoping morphed into steering. I've been writing all these poems; glum, but trying to be *good*, making snow angels in the paper—isn't that 'technique'? "Be good in the poem, be good." Isn't this some kind of dying, too?—The body, only a wound with potential? Is it really true? Does a victim make a victim? What if every season rises and falls and what remains is the year?

3. *What to Do Now With the Poem?*
after Diane Seuss' "The Other"

When I said to him, "let's go watch some boats this weekend", I'd hoped for nothing in this weather, but for the trees to be bare without their proper season; for direct comparison of how something can touch water, move through it without harm, eventually non-refundable.

I wrote a poem for my father's birthday, once, and he cried about it. My cigarette didn't taste right that evening, but I still smoked it up to the filter like I had deserved it. It all adds up to karma, doesn't it—the way you leave someone either disassembled, assembled—or both, all at once.

3.1 *The Abstract*

Sometimes, I think of language as a fool. You need its atoms for a sadness—the moan, the panting sigh.

In an almost-ode to Henry, that I wrote in Holland, on a real chesterfield couch—entirely in Arial, no abstract would stick to what I'd written. We're not similar, not even related—thank god. It was so long—the couch and the poem, about so long ago, I'm fascinated by how therapy didn't really do the trick.

Usually,
there's a Drive Through   down the street, and my hair

 is long enough to make it.   I'd see myself 'round midnight

in a bullseye, sewing mesh.   Nebraska

below the hands—true   megalomaniacs.

But I haven't seen a bird
like that since March.

(On to maybe happier thoughts.)

3.2 *Who is Speaking?*

Fact is, a line, touching someone else, is oftentimes an act of swallowing pride.

I'm not going to lie,
I have been other people.
Although, my business is my business.

There have been other people. This one ex—two days before Xmas, we talked on the phone and he told me, without detail, that he'd met someone else. I asked, if they had kissed—as if *that* was the big no-go, and the thought of investment in another woman, without actual bodily investment would mean we're just dandy—and hung up before he could answer. He could have texted it, morse coded it on the doorbell, could have telegraphed or faxed.

And would I have been cruel?
Would I have made him kiss her
for shock value? For clean cuts?

        Make out, have sex—there was a time I would;

the truth is so emotional—intelligence, too;

behind the speaker, guess who's speaking?—

3.3 Maybe I'm Ill, to Write ...

... while the lupins are thriving, damn all
has grammar. I cannot *really* name a thing.

Me, being what shape the air whittles of me, I fill myself with the chips of my spirit—follower
I've always been—the same-
doer. I'd set the table neatly with its contents
I'd like to live
to the letter.

That one night, I snuck around in the kitchen while my husband was snoring on the sofa, adding milk and flour to the dough in succession. And the butter boiled because, dear, I forgot I had it on the stove. I remember wanting to write a poem about it, but how I then said to myself, "not everything is a poem, darling!"—entitled to the word *darling*, talking to my almost-thirty, know-nothing-yet-self. My shocking(ly), many selves only mean well.

But in this room, as much as it is stick and stone,
there are flat leaves on the lakes;

I kiss you—and what labour.

3.4 Bigger than Before

I saw the plane rush out of the riverpalm and had nothing else in mind but the blueprint of a duck. Reverse-engineering is what they call it, I guess. To search for the natural in the premeditated—the vulnerability in the immortal.

There is a photograph of my husband and I, dancing by ourselves on the summer terrace, out where we had our wedding reception. The light is dim—just enough to glimmer onto the confetti balloons our friends had strung up, the silver *congratulations* garland, and the polaroids, pinned to the jute ribbon that was hung across the wooden stillage my father had sanded and flamed—what a vulnerable thing even this is: to let you imagine this moment not as it was, but as it could have been.

Origin

Like the Men in My Family

He stood with cotton like you would in a bathroom,
dipping seam into fabric,
like my grandpa would douse a swab in Carmol
and dab it on my forehead.
He stood and weaved a glove before work, and one after.

Behind the field there was a road like there would be behind light,
like there would be to a picture.
And if we took the road, we drove in an old Honda.
And if we drove in a Honda,
there was mother's perfume beneath the throttle,

there was a B&B, too, where on its roof was a telescope,
and I could watch the darkness.
He said, *the night has a long way to fall, like it wants to persuade the heart.*
And he continued to place woodworms
in the telescope like you would clean a wound, or build a star.

In the room, there would be a pillow under the gun
like a fly would be a fly
at first and spark fire at night. He stood there next to the pillow
like a safehouse, about to be abandoned,

took the bullets leaving the barrel like you would a scarf. He said, *you used
to hang upside down from a branch and the world
looked so much like it does now.* He said, *here. I have some silk-
worms to nest in your barrel,* handing me his prosthetics, gap-less

and white. And if I remember correctly,
I remember it like you would pour milk from a bull.

I Dreamt I Visited My Mother in Her Garden

The sun had sunk like her eyelids, into an afternoon. Her glasses, in an answer to light, allowed for her to see me, as if I were a photograph—a sepia picture; still young, like we had no history. We sat by the pond, on the low, marble stools. Every now and then, our bodies had so little worry, a bird would come to wash. She nipped on her water. Doused the hydrangeas with a can, split in its throat and I thought of what healing we could teach, even artificial things. The soil uncurdled from clump to cream, much like the Beta Blockers and Xarelto in her damp, whisking palms, much like our minds have, since birth, and then to clot again, in age.

Sixteen Songs for the Catbird

The night after your birthday, I dreamt I visited you in Colorado,
which was a field in New York City, wet

as a mountain's top, after a storm had opened
and ran across the crowds of seven

lives we had brought here—
everyone we have been, everyone

we gave to a future. Everyone we are
because of how our mothers have loved us.

& I forgot her face,
I bit into my own voice—hungry for myself.

If you walked down all of the streets of New York,
it would take a little over one hundred days,

and you'd arrive again & again at the little finger
of time & ask for one more way

to know yourself. Cut Colorado's mountains with a swiss pocket
knife into Switzerland six times one night & eat

their one thousand peaks by dawn.
Back in your apartment, which was a loft

in Midtown Manhattan,
your love was lying in their jeans and t-shirt

in a puddle of Cepheus' light pouring
through the skylights in the middle of the kitchen,

just feeling the light in my body being held by itself
& even though I had prepared

for it until it had become aftercare,
I still wore my mother's outfit, her rings & makeup.

& I know what I took that plane for, why I came to Colorado
in midnight's baffle.

Why I tied my sheets in knots & hung them
to be your front door. To climb those high shelves

in your kitchen, a catbird in my hands, an olive branch
of my own hair & jump into the flood.

Acknowledgement

Again, you see a shrub
in wind & think.
From your green
chin falls colostrum
& vaccine
onto your mother's chest.

Laissez-Faire

All july's so laissez-faire;
clouds cast
their dark nets like apostles
of grief, & a tongue's shade, too,
can fall both ways:
paisley on felt,
or hibiscus on mohair—
there's always the saying
& then, the softness
that doesn't want to.
It's a lot of guesswork—
the botanics of the body;
today, I walked as
elderberries' blossoms filled the zebra
crossing like a horseback
I was riding
& I recall an article
on flies with nowhere
to land but a seam-
less lion. A strand
of prairie. Walked to my mother's
house, to wait
again in her hip bone
like Lazarus. There in her garden,
I sat on my own chair instead.
I said, *I know, I should be blooming.*

Counting Sheep

Haven't been writing lately. Barely know how
it goes; it rained today, and I've somehow to make it
spectacular. I could make it stop, and you'd never know—
would you, about the buoys that came through
the manhole covers, the reddish, leaking car beforehand,
and the sand-covered street afterward. How my father
pulled a canister of oil out of the waves
at the wild beach in—was it Murcia? And my husband,
who stood on the shore with another, dented and empty—
reddish, just like that car, or if you're desperate
for something beautiful: a sunset behind the dunes.
I've got more memory than imagination.
The car we'd been driving—old, AC not functioning,
but a good car nonetheless, shook and swayed
in the wind that one day—that must have been in Murcia,
too, and it was just like it is today—I couldn't tell
the light from a cloud, the rain from a wave.
In the birdhour I was at my worst—
what a stupid phrase!—There were birds.
I was terribly bad at all hours. Which is why
I was in Spain in the first place.
With enough distance, I remember
what my mother said, and the way she chose to say it:
One day, we both went out for groceries,
when she drove off the main street and onto a dirt road,
until we stopped in front of a herd of sheep, or
"I haven't sung for you in a while—barely know how it goes."

The Learned Lover

Poem with Lines from My Grandmother's Phone Call/
Ekphrastic Poem after a Fantasy of a Man Dancing on Water

His Water Walz is a black and white photograph

being coloured in by my mother. The one

her father drove to take in the next village

in their family car, back in the 70's.

        He's drawn to the city, what can I say.

He moves like the fumes

of arrival—loneliness has come

to him & he is dancing in its headlights

as if to say, *come closer, I dare you.*

        His place by the window is always empty.

I am sure there is no boat, but if I'm wrong,

there is a nail & a hammer & hip bone.

There is skin & lacquer & woodworm,

bird & beak. That way, he is self-

sufficient, autonomous & ash.

He slurs the surface with his fingers,

just above the fishbodies & frogspawn.

What he takes, he gives back double—cries,

lets the water fall back

into itself, round & rippled.

Then, he presses his hands into it

like into the small of a back, until

skin floods over itself.

What kind of longing does my presence create

in him, that he looks for more

of my substance elsewhere?

I am still lonely.

It will be evening before he comes home. *Should I*

make soup, will you come hungry

from dancing? What nibbled toe

will I have to mend?

Ode to the Spit Sip

Early summer sinks like a good song
      back into the radio.
The forks were mine,
      but the lilac falls,

and I find new ways to kiss him—
eat from his spoon at night.

I've run from this kind of longing
like throttle from gas—
this small love

vow, this disgusting little glory.
But the dust has settled

on my curls, their wordless-long
journey through his hands—

we've touched all there is to touch.

Kummer Aufsatz

When the night is a young man,
the maples down the street stand like dust-blue thistles—I forget to desire, when we make love, I go to bed early, wake my husband up from work.

In between, I dream of the woman who drank her absinthe clear, and then another—clear, and then said in her voice, "I've not had anything but a salad today!", and now, I've said it, "desire."

The snow on his face,   and then the crocus

of his nose—   through and through.

I want to pinch   a nostril, so

it spells my accent in english
back to me;

to remember my own desires—who do you think of,

while you are gone?

Who do I call, if I desire you?

Even these alleys and their roofs: kissing
mouths of air, too moist to fall.

I'm barely sensitive, anymore
to this desire that life has for itself—its naked arms of light, orgies of wind.
Am not a good lover, either—too lazy to kiss the bodies in the crowd, the skins of air and longing.
Mother says, my hair is long, and did I want it that way. I say in my voice then,

"I want to twist

the doorknob of an ache, and enter."

I remember pain, and I remember the theft of it—the stockholm syndrome.
That glass face—a clear green, too—how it would reflect me, understand.

And my brain then, lavender in the tusk. Who do I ask for life

to drug me until I'm sick? If it rains,

it is often in bits of god—everywhere, the hunter of fugacity! When I cried,
it was often creation; sadness shed seven years long, and then another,
another seven, to pick up a life of its own—it is my skin. My skin that it walks in.

Nothing came to replace it. Nothing

aches. I'm lonely in this body. I need

the company of a feeling. For sadness to return
in chin-short hair, with new shoes and desires.

I'm drawing, again—my rosehip

tea like a blueprint for my amygdala.

What can it give me, but a stone

that holds life in its heaviness?

I'll have everyone call me

desperate for it.

Regrettably,

this ark—my deaf gazelles,
all heart broken
of kiss and condensation.
In the grass,

I never knew where I went.
Just this June, I grazed
my mirrors—green fangs
of the summer I loved

Bermuda shorts, and no one
came looking.

Piano Quai[1]

Zink-Licht meißelt mein Gesicht, schnitzt [2]
yin unter meine Lippen; du beobachtest mich—[3]
Xylograph (selbst du, ein Endoskop).[4]
Wieder, mit meinem Harz spielt die Nacht [5]
verstreichend Bratsche & der Klang [6]
un-erfindet & stellt wieder her die [7]
Trittleiter des Vogels. Im Garten- [8]
schuppen schweigt selbst das [9]
Radio. Du baust einen [10]
Quai in das [11]
Piano. Ich sehe zu wie das Licht von [12]
oben von alleine fällt.[13]
Niemand klatscht für einen Vogel, [14]
mehr als ein Vogel selbst, im nieder- [15]
Luft-Flug— [16]
kühn, in der Mitte des Augusts. [17]
Jetzt sag doch, [18]
ich sehne mich nach Liebe, während ich liebe. [19]
Hier sind wir: schwer [20]
gewachsen mit Redundanz Wer wär' [21]
fähig zu vergessen, die Nacht ist ein Jahrhundert, [22]

[1] **Piano Quay**
[2] Zinc-light chisels my face, whittles
[3] yin beneath my lips; you watch me—
[4] xylograph (even you, an endoscope). Again,
[5] with my rosin, the night plays
[6] viola fleetingly, & its sound
[7] uninvents & remanufactures a bird's
[8] trestle ladders. In the garden
[9] shed, even the
[10] radio is silent. You build a
[11] quay into the
[12] piano. I watch the light above fall
[13] on its own.
[14] No one claps for a bird
[15] more than a bird
[16] low-flight—
[17] keen, mid-August.
[18] Just say,
[19] *I long for love while I love.*
[20] Here we are:
[21] grown heavy with redundancy. Who'd
[22] forget the night is a century,

egal wie schnell. In meinem Traum, lechzt selbst [23]
der Hügel über den [24]
Campern danach ein [25]
Berg zu sein & wer klatscht & klatscht, wenn nicht das Flussbett? [26]
Auf & kondensiert, schon irgendeine Wolke. [27]

[23] even if quick. In my
[24] dreams, even the hilltops above the campers,
[25] crave to be mountains, & who, if not the river-
[26] beds clap & clap?
[27] Already evaporated, already some cloud.

Song for George

I find my blessings
       in his

                hip bone & sing
& sing again, tomorrow.

His gender, moon-
       age softened & feather

to the cry of my given nature.
      I am no hope,

               I step away from my own prayers
    like the silent return of an ambulance.

He is no lighthouse, he is
what becomes of its light—

      the rescue, the bell.
Therefore I am movement

          & below his chest
   I listen.

His eyes are not water,
      they are what makes the water

     chant
of its voyage, the salt

        that licks the boat-rim
into crystal, Amethyst—

how it calms
   itself

& then me, & me again,
tomorrow.

He fishes, nets
     even the stones

            from their groundwork:
      sometimes he comes to me half-hipped

& lonely,
skin like afternoon moon-sight.

I make his mouth this way:
pull with my thumb

at his jawbell & ring & ring
       for another blessing.

       He barks *Baby, we have sinned.*
Baby, metal again & *Baby*.

I fall to his feet in thanksgiving,
offer my backbone as a cane

for his tongue.
       His mouthsweat holifies

            what cross it carries—
               if loneliness is a sin,
then we have made it our love.

Esther

With the birds
in your hair—those fly
abouts, you've become what a year

exchanges for another—
their monogamised
distance

and the ferry
in me that thinks
of you from harbour

to harbour, desires
deep seas. I attempt
to look at the sky and not see

the beast for a bird
just because it needs
to carry its own wings.

Your scholarship
at the living thing,
the doing thing—

has it expired? What better
for a mouth to do
than to undo. Your hair

falls south, the birdbath
here, on the terrace.
I haven't heard from you

until just now.

Engine Study in Oil

I remember the rooibos
in your hair—drunken
on and milky. Shy sermon
of flowers,

how they preach their own
beauty, and yet forget
about it. I've called
this a blessing: to drive

my fingers down that lined
page at night, and re-
create each round top
with a tittle. Large night,

bright truck; the driver
(even I desert myself
here), a southpaw
smoker—all my yellow

paint, my golden pair
of compasses, used up
on a hand, holding—
what? The disco ball

in the driver's compartment—
your eyes like spilled salt.
Look over my shoulder.
Look over my shoulder—

in the bedroom,
the gown hangs heavy

over the door, we're both
dreaming of things that stay.

Within Origin

Are my hands abstract
to your body, yet?
How long has it been
since you last grappled grief
without grieving?
And love?
Is it bluegill season,
or carp? Let me touch
you like a salmon
in a pond.

Conservatory

Nothing happened in the fantasy—his skin is still full
of harps. It's raining, outside the birdbath like an open
chord. It's because he's all fact; a time-worshipper.
I make room in the piano, for the skin that falls
when he rises and enters the day, slim body, tight
shirt. I missed how he took another slice of pizza,
could've fooled me for a loop—probably some saturday,
around the same time as now. His beard is making
sentences with full recipes, I've run out of flour—what dough
to press against it? I said, *c'mon, let's do some yoga!*
Miscalculated the small life a downward dog leads.
In his sleep, I grind my teeth for him
like pearls in the mussels
of his ears. Last night we stayed
in, and when I woke this morning, the house reeked
of cooked meat. I've put the roses on the grill
so it's still August, when we wake.

Dear George

Last night, the rain disturbed with its funeral; I needed
the routine of watering the plants—above the coffee
machine hung my daily schedule: *brush teeth, walk
dog, write.* It fell like a scale, my fruitless optimism

enlarged behind the water tank,
as if to point out my non-accomplishments.
Its music, penurious; my small

life not in chaos—chaos, too, has a beat.
Rather do I know these engines, too, must grieve
what they cannot carry. I think you know just how heavy
a dead kaleidoscope is. But I confess: I've danced

in a eulogy—I'm not exactly certain where I am.
I know the planet, know the country. For years
I've cried in this body, but the chin still fears me.
There is an echo, just after a tear escapes the eye, ashen.

Like a windbell calling for silence. I could see myself,
hopeless—a cloud in water. I haven't paid any attention
to where the sun gives up on the day. Even after the rain,
the cars drove past and through, *rewind* and *rewind.*

But we stood out on the terrace, August had left
the house warm. It was late as the streetnoise dried,
after we'd been so close,
we were almost air, and we saw Jupiter, lit up

like a southern star, where each year, the cranes
must come rattling in with their horns of sunlight

and my mind could have gone
anywhere but chose to stay right there.

Chronology Dice

The open window performs
the sound of an accolade—

the sword of water against the chain-
armoured shoulder of a shore

& through the curtain
of his slouched back, his ribcage

grows like a cut pear—*you must have
two cores*. Below him, I'd call myself

*farmer & telescope
picker*. This table turns

down my adrenaline, flat
like the ribbon

of his hip bone.
The advantage is no one's & this is fair

because my chest is at his chin
& heartbeat drips best like slow honey.

My voice lowers to scooter and skid
around in his earshell—Saturn's wedding

band around his tragus, eighty-two
moons half lit

into innovation by his face—he's the smartest
man I know. The devil on his nape

is mortal as sin—its nature is to die
in the posture

of our forgetting
& O, how he has not forgotten

but forgiven mine.
He smells my belly's soft, lavender

rows of my ribs. The hieroglyphs
of his nostrils, birdwide

& then a folded wing, a balding
bow towards extinction

with only the legacy
of my scent. My collarbones,

an upside down pyramid. Above it,
the Nile runs into his mouth.

Jukebox

It's been two years, and the step
from terrace into the garden

is still not covered with wood.
Weeds rush into the gravel

like rats, and thinking of it,
rats most likely do, too. Dandelions

have fully fledged—the summer
we had screwed and hammered

the floorboards down, his hair was still
a little more chestnut than grey,

and each white bird was like a jukebox
in it. He said then, almost whistling,

he'd do it. But then it rained
and under those streetlamps from across,

the way he was standing
he was being filled with coins and coins.

Tomorrow, he sang. When we
stood all dressed up at the civil service,

and the clerk asked *do you?* And he replied,
I do, I knew he'd meant forever.

Memo for the Reader

I long to carpent a door
just to say something in passing.
How the sand in mother's hair draws out the smoke—
for just seven minutes or so
I sit out on the porch at night with a lit
cigarette. What I can't remember, I imagine:
the moon, a glaucoma in the night.
How mother's been trying to get me to quit
and so far I've quit everything
but writing, but love, but smoking.
I wish for you to read this poem
on your way to the next,
and for me to say,
the way I'd loved him
was, as if the grasshopper of
my imagination was fickle as a stone,
like telling you, your mother called
last night, it was important.

The Learned Crop

To the Carnivores in Spotted Treelight

      Your birch, in the twilight
      of rain; a tall, wet
dog, but gorgeous. You'd time

      only an eon; laugh into a piano-
      like root, and even this fine
yeast will become a distance

      I'll forget like air—even my father's
      house, against my mother's skin—
a roughcast wedding dress. Saw it twirl once,

      in spotted treelight, or felt it and forgot:
      this kind of rain throws over a stranger's voice
only to taper it into a body

      that looks like a sparrow swinging in wind
      chimes, until air forgets like air—what is not forgotten?—
Alien, even air asks your wing, *O, where to*

      with this body, where from? Thought
      you were a philanthropist, Armageddon,
      I am
herewith your basket. Who knows, how far your feathers fall

      and forget which bird they've come from,
      like air, until we write with them.
The moon dusts the streets each dark. Your tower-

      eyes—each one: a wet button—
      slide backwards through silk
into their closet of skull,

      the way he slipped his body into his red car,
      and all forget (so easily)—the song,
uneaten, as if to prepare

      for something to exist first. I've written my name
      as *Angelica*, meaning hologram. Think,
how the cicadas refrain

        from you, who lends them melody, and so a song about
           your raid becomes a dirge. We live, mostly, by remembering
each other's names. How we live, is whether we can remember

        our own. Your birch's tears will
           themselves to be worms without cause
or mouths even—my face looks

        like just a face. I look like
           I've never heard a bee rattle
against a window. I sit in the hairline

        of a threshold like a blind
           chameleon—incapable
of age.

Darius, I've Stopped Imagining Things

In the motel room,
I see my mother's flares, two-stepping

in the curtains. My dad's perm
in the carpet-

chunk, lifted by the skirting
boards that widen towards the corner:

the left trumpet sleeve of my mother's tie
dye shirt—if I put my hands into the hairspray

slings like hers—splinter
and nail, touched his face

against the clock, the floor would turn chestnut
and I would still be
copper. The 70's

came here a little late;
Dancing in the Dark plays: old lightbulbs

skim my body, draw assumptions
of movement onto the wall.

A mattress, acoustic
like their Manta's reclined

back seats, seven cable
bracelets around the elbow

of a lamp—the light of my father drives
in the yellowed shade.

Tussles, like the curve
of his receding hairline.

My mother's crochet top hangs in the door
window of the bathroom. A joint

she swears never to have smoked
is stacked by the sink; rolled soap, lit

white, bubbling—
My mother keeps her long hair.

The delivery room blossoms twice
with blue balloons, budding-

basin haircuts and toy cars
like a pebbled path to the play room.

I have not even been a kiss, yet.
When you call
with an unknown number,

there isn't anyone here
to imagine it's you.

Memoir of a Twerk, Read to a Dark Room

in the evening, i drag myself
out of god's deathbed.
        ask, *did u love ur mother*

enough to imagine her? do i still exist irl?
& tell my mom to pls stop calling me
        a child in her prayers. he says, *woman,*

with a violence that, 7 yrs later, in the changing
room at *bridal dream* i will still see: the ribs
poking
        out as if to make another human being

from myself. i walk again, the zinc
        streets of his acne
chest, after dark & in those blue stilettos

of my fingertips. there's a field
        4 this kind of thing: even his hip—
a seizure in mine.

o, home-made boyship,
        wyd? it's dark here,
read the room. y the mouth

full of rain, hänsel?
        y the crouton
in the birdbath?

sb was me yesterday.
        felt all the things
& brought nothing home.

here's a fact,
        without reason
to believe it:

u r both, comet & dinosaur.
        some ppl don't believe in evolution, u know.
s/w (on youtube)

i looked for glue
& paper. held arms
   to hips like a screw clamp.

my laptop on the laundry
basket, a video
   on *how to twerk* full screen

as if for the light
to outgrow darkness lol. i can't dance
   to save my life

& i can't expect much from this air.
i prayed, *god, this ass*
would look so fine if it could twerk,
& god, this body would feel so good if i felt it.

Eye Training

Mother says, I could train my eyesight with a pencil;
switch from macroscopic vision to the dog's

height in the doorway, the Halloween candy
you'd always eat. And I've tried.
And tired. To break the pendant
of his touch—to snap out of this seeing.

Then, blue stone-eyes roll sideways, open the grave—
fold the sheets and bandages for me,
I haven't the heart to tell God I am risen
without him.

                                                      —I watch you
                                                      watch tiktoks, chuckle

                                       an applause so heron flight low,
                            the fish in the tank open their chest

                                   of bubble machines to use air
                   as their decoy. You angle the phone towards

                                            me, show me the blue
                     garden where your Nan used to live.

                                Say, *look babe! Charmouth Beach.*
                             I take your phone, roll the stones

                                       back into their place
                           of prophecy and train my eyes

imagining. When I park my car by the chestnut
                 tree, next to a red Toyota the following
                 day, I put the visor up and see Jesus wear
                        my prayer like a sequin dress

                   of fishing hooks, stand on the water
                   drops of terraces I once saw in Turkey
                   that resembled God's eight billion
                 earshells, now on my windshield,

                         where he stops believing
                  that he can, and starts sinking.
Or simply light—the shape of an upside-
                     down leaf, signified by it.

Autumn unburdened and untethered
from its connotations:
angels fall, we reciprocate
their shape in winter

as if to say, *you have merely changed us.*

Kummer Feld, Kummer Gericht

If you are grief   then you are also an envy
            of heaven   Because Ruben's   first son was the last
of 256 and I imagine   that to be your father's name   106 had already died

              before you and I give you just that fateful minute   to ask your stepmother
          about your labour   The memoir
of her full breasts When I am thirty

                              my mother will have told me about the women
                      in the communal showers   in Russia
About their breasts   hanging like ripe fruit   She will have said

         how they tossed the sucking   of their children behind their ears
into the bowl   of their collarbones   like a child's
leaving was a gravity   they could hold   to wash

                              what naked hunger is underneath
Your stepmother will say   we danced   in your absence
              because her breasts are firm   and her nipples   small and you

          after all   are grief
loud sorrow   murderous
You never had straight A's in school   got fired from your cashier's job

              But you do sideway clamps on the bar   of every lamppost
     When you leave   when you expire on my thirtieth
              birthday   I will sew pearl and sequin into your beard When you lay

above me like an upside down field   I will dress you in the satin   blouse you unbuttoned
   cover your shaven   chest hair   your empty harvest   I will weave
              gerberas into the hay   of your scrotum   Walk to the courtroom

of your navel   and say   *he has not killed me*

On Birds

I.

                Papa just misses a pigeon
      with a hopscotch-rock,

& that is the way being named "hope"
carries its burden. Then, grandma's fingers
             pinch
                my flawless cheeks like salt. She drafts

a boat
from her lips, singular, preoccupied.
              When I tell her I don't like it,
we're on Hainan
              & I don't have anywhere

              but water. Mama's colleague
knows who
I'm in love with
              & cuts off my ponytail,

              but Mama still wants to be
best friends. I wake early the next day
to find myself
a daughter. We raise

              chicken for their fragility,
& Frida sleeps on Mama's pillow,
but follows
      me around

the garden.
              Mama sews me a skirt
to wear to church. The seam
only kissed the sewing

machine
        & after the sermon
it confesses like wings
that lay bare their frame with each flight.

             That means, Mary might not have been
a virgin. That means a mouth
can be piece
                    and blackmailer at the same time.

II.

                The fan drags a dead bird/
hot air/ thirty three degree Celsius
around with its propeller.
Through the window,

                the coral
dies by the hands of white
            curtains & it reeks
of coconut conditioner, oxygenated

                    drinking water & seventy
             nanograms of bad girl
                    testosterone; half a bridge
             on a foot.

                    & I give her what girls want
             which is attribute/
feature/ distinction/ contribution.
             That means, I hand her

the chalk
        she fingers me
with. That means, we are now
             in contrast—

the words *friends* or *lovers,*
             not animalistic enough.
        The dead bird picks at her shadow,
a chisel, however pragmatic—there to carve,

studies the stone. Rehearses its reverse,
        makes an organ of a stimulus
in a God's pubescent flair.
             A chip of hair loosens

        from its bun.
I ignore the jewellery—
the heart-
             pendant & diamond

ring—best
while wearing it.
& I give her what girls want
    which is a secret/

    non-cursive/ abstract/ seven minutes.
That means, I give
her a closet.
  That means, I hand

her mother a picture
of a boy & don't write anything in my diary.
That means, she has
  long hair & no tower
but my cervix.

The Coroner's Hairbrush

The falcon, a single wire,
and beneath it, my nostrils
once pigeonholes, now tourniquet
for your Old Spice.
When I forget where I am,
the greyhound waits
in the lilac bed
of your nails.
Come on astronaut,
send me another message   on MySpace
    just to know   you're far
    away,
    just to flag   you even further.
Icarus could not hold anyone,
and I wish myself a sun
where I don't have to.
Let's walk down the body in question:
hair; question. Desire; imagination—
        what happens when the country
                leaves the countrymen?
Does my self prophecy apply to you?
There are those kind of love songs
that are sung in the threshold
of bathroom doors,
      there are those kind of bristles
          on your wooden chin
              that are the coroner's
hairbrush—so simple, yet so accomplished   at adding volume to death.

Lover says: to lust for life is one thing.
Lover says: to die for it is another,
and clearly, the Mountain here has come
to Moses—mornings I kneel by his bedside
into the *I Do* of air, like into a valley
        and say, *move me, move me.*

Hunting Season

I know what it hunts—the air.
A neighbour mows the lawn
and the scent is inescapable.
The rain comes like hounds,
their round snouts sniffing the grass.
I see a horse-like cloud:
a magnet in the sky —it turns
and the dogs evaporate;
all the foxes, still here.
All day yesterday, I could feel
something between my thighs;
thickening air, a former lust.
Abracadabra cerebrum,
a bird confides on its flightless
days in paper, as do I.

Forgive the Window

He poured milk into his cereal—I could
have asked then, *what light has hurt you?*
and gotten my answer. Could have said, *hey!*
What age did you find your father
fitting his prosthetics with milk
teeth?—but I didn't. And then, the next
day came, and the next; a kind of ocean
that does not return to shore. I want to make him
human like this; outlivable and small.
Prone to disease, heart failure, karma.
I'm afraid, I am a god. Letting him live
in me like this. I am almighty
in therapy, impotent in the rocking chair
by the open window towards the driveway.
Whatever remains untouched
by the weather, we must eat last—
I fell in love, moved and got married.
Said, *soon I'll get fixed. I'll try therapy again.*
Forgive the window, late night. The merciless
comparison, but the cryer's out in me. I've
talked when I wasn't ready.
If there is a right way to touch me,
even I, in my illusion, have done it wrong.

Brushsmith

That maple leaf shows on your ribside;
a fallen hand, outlawed

from heaven. Do I believe
that she loved you?—Sure, but she was young,

and we're all stupid when we're young.
You plucked its stem

like country from continent—
flew to Australia

to live in a van,
& made of it a council

of bristles. Covered your credit card
details with the shade of your broke-ness

& painted yourself
a friend with a guest room.

Shaved your long hair,
blueish black, like a fish in water.

That shoestring necktie
that fits you like a ferrule around

your collar, crimps
when you laugh. & when you still wore braces,

God knows, the Orthodontist hammered
wear your goddamn elastics

into your teenage head, so you'd know
how to use it as a nail—

that rhubarb eye, the fruitless
sun & the chaos below it

now hangs in our parents' house
& I wonder how my truth

has always been an act of disappearing
instead, dreadful and still

warm. Last summer you pierced
an eardrum

of paint with an electric guitar
& the sound

was beautiful.
& when you told me about a man

who injected himself with E. coli
& directed his breath to black out

the windows
in his veins. When you told me

there wasn't a shadow on the wall
of his stomach, I endure

another heartbeat. I believed
in the snow

slit beneath the tyres,
the arrival at innocence

without melting it. I drove home
just to have something crawl

underneath the headlights
& back into the woods.

Tristan

We'll celebrate whatever
    snow-ridden day it is,

when I can only speak riverwater.
    When I step on my tonguebed

and the rocks are round.
    We'll go to the botanical gardens

and I'll water the succulents
    on your chest

with my spit. Say
    with high humidity, *here, have me like*

you knew I was coming.
    You didn't grow a beard to hide

your mother's face beneath it—
    how did she love you? And doesn't it make you

sad—the definiteness of "did"? I can't remember
    what my father said about love,

but I remember his tears
    when I moved out and on.

The thing is, he didn't know what I left—
    that fact made me want to become him.

The thing is, when he found
    out, my name sounded

funereal.
    Some of my body's light still catches

the truth of that house.
    When my bones rupture

with laughter, my flesh doesn't know
    the difference of a good bleed and a bad

man. Some say, *coping mechanism*
    and how strong it made me.

   I am not talking about my father,
I am talking about Tristan—

   that, of course, is a made-up name,
because when I tell the light

   my tongue falls out like
my story doesn't belong to me.

(I wonder what his purpose was,
now he's in my body,

he doesn't even talk, doesn't
tell me what happened.)

   This is now third nature,
one I have been served

   on the rusted platter
of my bed. The oil stain

   of his body engine, grease
I have taken to white-coated

   strangers, like to the public
washing machines, sat and waited

   for an hour worth a coin,
worth 50 dollars. Came out

   wet and heavy. Isn't that what it is like,
to talk about trauma, doesn't it traumatise?

   Heaven held its birds and songs
and hallelujahs above my head,

   they say, which only meant I was dead-
flat on my back like a bug.

   I have now learned to flee
but it is only from my own self

   and into your rib bones. But whose heart
wouldn't want that. Look, I don't want to injure

love with my knowing-nothing-about-it.
I don't want to spin an empty

barrel at a rabbit, I want you to chew
on the led when you make a meal

of my hunting. Lose a tooth for a heart,
you thief. I mean to say that out loud

to my father and have him be done
grieving my name. Love is such a colossal

question, and for some reason
this poem is not about Tristan at all.

The Learned Water

Portrait of His Love as a Widower

If Michael Jackson's nose hadn't fallen off,
there would be snow, falling
from your hip bone. You'd lay
in your own identities like a selfmade angel

and wait until spring to ask, *are we innocent?*
You've dyed your hair, and I grieve

and grieve you again,
but you still don't know
who you are. Long live Lazarus, the missing people
of New York City. Their prelude bodies

we pull from rivers
and into headlines—here, there is no water

for your many evolutions.
If Mona Lisa had eyebrows,
you could at least have been honest
in therapy. Elementary School You

plucks them into two
thin condolences, but now, bushy

brows are in. Here, you are not found
by anyone but yourself,
and there is still hope.
There is no bridge

to set fire to—darling,
my mother gave me nothing

and in return I gave you steel. O, motherly
bullet, childhood
inadequacy—and how tragic, how terribly
nothing at all: your dying is never

permanent, yet my grief
has doubled. Your ash falls like dice

in the car park behind the Consum—
you are a tree

without a forest, even though
I am here. You've dyed
your hair again, and I grieve
and grieve.

Eons

to P.

The eons, hiding in your curls. Once you had braids,
and a minute was so true. What genesis, when you woke

from yourself, like cornsilk wakes the ear. Not a single
pollen in your beard now. I got up this morning

and the sky was green. I could walk towards you
on this paper. I could walk towards myself.
My mother laughed last night

and this morning, I see it still
like an eternal bird. I want to offer it
an ear, better than those on my head.

There were lilies on the coffee table,
and I had to write. I feel nothing
I've lived leaves without a fight.

I'd write without thumbs, on the computer—animalistic,
how could we hold anything but inside our mouths?
I've missed your poems, P., and I haven't figured out

why my energy to write has been so low. I should have asked
your address, screens have a way of making things eternal,
and I want you to read this question in the dark:
what, in daylight, could the moth desire?

To The Streets of Hong Kong that Glisten with Their Sadness

for Kika

Even with the fabric
of curls, I would tilt
my head around in Eden & into her bell—-
& lovers would come like this—
as if through, to the generation
of their own mother—
& go like this.
I've not invited
the tree to the knife, nor
my flip phone proof into
the toilet to become a taxidermist
of my accent, or to drown it.
I'll just continue: with short hair,
I talked even more
like my mother. Shaved
the head by the side, & after the funeral
I'd cut the curls willy-nilly. My point is,
that now, she's been calling
weekly & even on holidays.
Meanwhile, all my devils are glass-
eyed, even in the drawers
in the bedroom.
Three years, my hair's been growing.
I had an up-
do for my wedding—I don't want to leave
anything to chance, so last week I ate
grapefruit with my antidepressants.

Last week, I dared my face out
by the hair—the chopped-off strands,
wet & stubby
like the shoes of a toddler. Same day,
I hugged my cousin, from my father's side,
  whose birthday it was
  & whose mother has arthritis
in all of her ten fingers, like my father does
in his wrist;
the strap of his scan
watch, as if my brother returned,
halfway to Costa Rica
with too much luggage.
  Held him there like my aunt would
hold a pair of gardening
shears, after her in-law mother passed.
The pain persists, as does the memory &
her fingers are figurines of this; a Salvador
Dali painting, that at fifteen, when I was still
straightening my hair
in Abbotsford November,
I wanted tattooed on the dais
of my shoulder blade.
She's the same aunt, who sewed the back
of my silver sequin dress down to my
shapewear in, I think, 2013? I left
his party I was poorly bartending
& that night my bladder thought
itself a psychic—did you shave the streets
  in your city? My knuckles look like
manhole covers on the sidewalk of a
finger—could you come through?
Into my palm-field of sweetgrass—lay
  what roads you've barbered
into the cow-lick of my elbow.
I'm whistling on our future, feeling
sad vs cowgirl.

Paperboy

Have you moved

much, since the half-trains that came and kept coming to your door? The horses
somehow sitting in the back. Evening's at five I'd boat

from room to room—O, to push

this steamship's fumes from europe to northamerica! Maybe it's because
I once ate one of my cousin's grapes, that when they'd come toward you, I'd reel

to you their entire gnashing.

I feel that it is noon between us, and how intimate
this gear—is it so terrible? My shim-like feet? I cried the first time boarded

their new function. Do we drink

the last sip of this consequence?—This industrialisation
of emotion? Put the milk on the stove and be jealous?

Went out and buzzed

his door, rang the bars along the windows like silver
orchards in the moonlight. Spiders moving through where the

hips should be, spinning

bones into this green field of a grape—from the curled wheat
between them, I bake the bread of my absence. Do I have to enter through myself

to get to him? There's a chin

to me, who will not run from it? Who will ever see me without?—Should
he touch me there, fold it like a paperboy, and again, forget

his skin on my flesh?

Saw two shapes on the sidewalk. The airbag like a mother's chest, and those same pearls
on his dresser. At home, I waited for the fly to drown, before

I called to tell you, I am not as dangerous

as other things. He must be tired of leaving his pain by the door.
Of the airplanes that come with letters, written on computers, of moving

from room to room on a conveyor belt.

Love in Particular

You still hear his hymns when the shower runs.
Say, *draw another branch into the storm, Love*, to no one
in particular, or maybe to the orthopaedic shoes, the dress
pants crouched over the chair.
Anything is at its most sincere while it is being
practised—the conduction of his Russian church
choir in front of these mirrors, the singing in the slim vase
of the hallway, until everyone was all set and ready
to go worship Jesus in Jerusalem. *Ya hochu kushat'*—
behind the shower curtains you catch his rolling
Rs like your sleepless body, and this rare rain
comes in drops the size of chickpeas, leaves the air as silk
as hummus, while you wash your hair with the honey
his life has left. *Ya hochu spat'*—since your night shifts
at the retirement home you can't remember whether you've slept
or not, which at best is the same thing as not sleeping.
So even in daylight you say, grandfather came to you,
pinched voices off the beach
until they were his choir. At the shore of the Dead
Sea—the infinity of your bathtub
that contains much too much bath salt to be skin-friendly,
all your prayers for this grief to become a stone
were unanswered. Here, what belongs in bodies
of water isn't there, what belongs on land
practises ascending. Here, where he could miss you,
you float to meet him halfway, on water that knows
to resurrect itself through thresholds and open windows
and fall back to where it belongs like pentecost—this roof
speaks in tongues of his absence and you don't know
who to call to fix it. O small Jerusalem
beneath your nails. Look how you've made yourself a place he'd love
to visit. Sing his name and make your mouth
a replica of the grave his faith rose from.
Every wall in your hands bends west:
you bury grandfather's photograph in the dark
circles of god's setting eyelids,
where he can be merciful. At Mount of Olives,
rising from the valley
of your orange bed sheets,
you weep and wash its feet with your tears,
feed their windy mouths with your chestnut
hair. *Say, wish you could see Jesus'*

agony still sticking to the trees
in Garden Gethsemane. I cannot wash it off? O Bethlehem
of your radiator by the dinner table—warm
womb of your faith, where he sat and read his bible
as if drinking milk. How do you visit without tears?
How do you not disown her of your belief,
when god has left you so terribly awake.

I Try Not to Place a Brow in

This is the fourth season—counting backwards, that I haven't heard from her. I'd met Madeleine in September, and left her there, too, eight years later by the Salines, red-brown and ribbed as her hair in rain. It's difficult to tell apart what the heart remembers, and what the head remembers. But still, memory is what returns without returning—no old leaf will come back in spring. Yet, the trees are patient. How much certainty in unreturnable friendship does it take, to delete each other's Candy Crush scores?

//

The night's black pepper falls. I'm up at 4 am and already self-improving; I watch a tutorial. How to *really* wear a slim fit shirt without looking like a fool—still in pyjamas and my husband's fleece dressing gown, because grief, today I haven't a muscle to clothe you. I want something. My sadness, too, wants something. I search for her the way air searches for a flute hole. I'm motivated to remember again, the ease of her face. A pond of hungry carp. Each sparkle of light, a flake to her freckles. Try not to place a brow in, a septum. The t-zone. There's this joke my father tells: "a sandwich walks up the stairs, realises it can't walk and runs back down again", and I live by it.

Review of an Ache

after Ocean Vuong's 'Beautiful Short Loser'

I started listening to Timberlake again, when I found out my aorta was a river with a backflow. I'm speeding through the gods I'd be— want it to become better acquainted with its future.
Who gives a shit how tall the trees are?— Sometimes my breathing chops my ribs up.
This is how you can surrender every bone in your body: climb your lover's stairwell.
Lately, I feel like dying is more severe than living. Maybe the same.
How crazy—I was standing on the wrong side of air. I found a god I can live with.
I throw the timbers into the lake by the aortic — ark, Noah?
The air is basically a limbo for water. I'm always on the verge of a heartbeat. Wanted it to know I'd still love—maybe even more so. The losing stays and the having goes. I said to my doctor, *how beautiful my laughter is when it is pulled out of these depths.*
I think, everything is gold but gold itself.
I also think: *Wiederkehr, Uhrmacher.* If the air is god's mood ring, it means I must be in the same mood as god.
My dog's favourite spot is in the hollow of my knee, I think it's because she secretly believes in prayer.
Bremsmittel, Herz-Verschleiß.
I googled the average length of a rib. The longest is 24 cm long. I've got some breath left, still.
I said to my doctor, *do you think he'll come back?*

What Do You Expect Me to Say, Clearly I was Disappointed

After Kaveh Akbar's 'Orchids are Sprouting from the Floorboards'

I'm a diamond kinda girl.
I say to my heart "love better",
and it becomes a diamond.
I say nothing to my friends
and they become diamonds.
I sleep naked
and my husband becomes a diamond.
I look at his face
and life becomes a diamond.
I cook soup for my mother
and she, too, becomes a diamond.
I visit your absence
and it becomes a diamond.

The Re-Learner

Dear Youth, I Dream Tonight in Arms that are Gentle

& what came to kill,

won't. When termites ate through the years

of the old pine tree, your mother

made a pesticide from your smoked

cigarettes & you knew to take it

as her testimonial.

It's not because

I'm scared, you know—

I swear it was that basketball

in seventh grade, that knocked

sadness into me. Bounced

nose-bone through the hoop

between my eyes, dislodged parts

of my brain & whenever

I have a lover,

there is an island between their thighs.

That's why everything smells

of dandruff, that's why every scent

is visible. There is no rush,

only rain in my arteries,

which teaches me

faithfulness is a routine.

Really, my body trying to adjust

to these pills, is a lot like learning to love.

I wish from them only onliness.

The sequel to desire is desire—

I am both,

your snow and threshold.
O apathy, what wingless moth
you had made me. Sometimes
I think I'm only heavy
so that I won't blow away.
There were swing sets
at eighteen,
there is a fire in the basement,
of your teens, and I have lost
my shape to air, but what can fight
hellfire better than air, leaving?
Between what breaks
and what withers, is my fear
of ownership—
tell me you're bipolar
without saying you're bipolar:
I'm only here for the excitement.

Canoe

Hey, I'm back. Came here closed   atlas, peppered
light—swung beneath a disco ball,   didn't feel it.
             Watched the robbery:
      everyone hunched
their hips   under the laserlight,
    smeared across their skin   like green
lipstick on St. Patrick's.   Didn't feel it
wear off.   Came here
because the street was pouched in light
       and I had no clutch
to go with my shoes, yet.
     Came here asking people   in whose image
you were made—   silly me, forgot
       you didn't have to be made twice
to be remembered.   Came here
and then the music   was clueless.
     Came here because the street lamps were low
pyramids—   so ancient,   but I still wonder
   who's the dust,   and   who's the museum
and   where   is   the dance floor?
Pre-electric light only had one   emotion:
a single longing to dissolve   in darkness—
came here because there was a silencer
screwed onto my lanterns.
Thought you might know   something
about the body   that isn't bodiless,
          that isn't
              somehow
                 a migration.
     Know I'm only soft
at a distance,   only brutal to myself up close.
I've got a blindfold
between my shoulders—   I only measure uneven
       5'6 but hear you've got a ladder,
    hear you're a forest and I'm returning
in my head-lit canoe.

Self-Portrait as Tinder

You part your hair zigzag again, so I can't ghost you.

I swipe across your scalp & perch on its dandruff—

it snows mid-August & I feel so super special

without my seasonal depression.
Had such small wavelength, no true imagination.
& so, I theorise about the green thumb

of my mother; the lilac pyramids in her front yard

& the headlights of her car, atomising

the dark. I was only myself, trying music—

who is only me
in motorised skin—& thought:
a pianist is only a prison

guard holding a key & thought, now this music

had made a good woman

of herself & still, you break my heart.

& so, I waited for it to rain
my lover's beard—he'd cut the hedge
& flushed the stubble.

Shaved the chin

into the wheelbarrow.

Roller skated to the street sign

with his razor—looked so boyish:
wish I'd known him. Found a neon
seed, a smoke of worms.

Found the stencil

of a six pack shape a lovesong

like a turtle—found it in his hair

like curlers,
& you got so jealous.

& so, the lanterns baptise
their light. I heard a god invent hibiscus
in Alaska, & it all happened in my body.

Pinched two things that exist

like they did not, & so now they're woke

like me: a praying

mantis on a popsicle—aren't you absurd?
Something outran my childhood like a cyst
on a kitten & it was just a prototype.

They tell me to fix it, or else—

& so, was my own death only fiction?

For everything behavioural

there's a thesaurus, there's archeology.
I couldn't hear god
think that day, couldn't replace it,

& so, the ferris wheel in my Babylonic

head, so the language. & so, you are

& aren't you a dynamo, spinning on air.
& aren't you just artificial grass in snow.

The Other Woman

The thing is, I was depressed
when my husband called me
his girlfriend—an accident
of the tongue.
I looked at our kitchen,
the spatulas and tableweeds,
dried out like a cloth,
said, "good god! I'm her,
aren't I?!"

If I Could, the River

Dear R.,

I'm sorry I've not mailed the letter.
Lately, the travelling of me; a bird that tunes

the worm. I've been paying attention, collecting.
Heard the beetle wing

of skin fold into his hip, figured folding
is how we know of each other. Hence, this letter.

Just this autumn, George in his grey slacks,
how not to listen to the hem cruise on the maples

like a jetski in the harbour—how not to kiss the convoy
of his elbow? Where to see him truly naked,

but in the boudoir behind his hairline?
Thinks only sometimes of his old basset and the scrunchies.

I'm not afraid to admit that I'm jealous.
I wear so many clothes, something for each occasion—

our new sofa came last night, and its scent
woke in me a desire. I hung the old frames, shampooed

the dog with my shampoo. Got my white corduroy culottes
and sat on the beige corduroy couch, expecting something.

In the psych ward, I'd walked like locusts
on a field, from old linoleum to new linoleum

and ended up just linoleum—
I know the bear, know so little of it, still.

If I could, the river's salmon.
To return to who I was and put down all my whereabouts.

The Good Summer

In my head, the dogyears.
There hasn't been anything absolute

for months. I've died
without vultures, the soul hung like rain; outward.

Beneath the seasons rests the year, as you rest
in your holed t-shirt, on the lawn chair—almighty

skin, eternal for now. If it were up to you, I could throw
out the lavender we keep in the cupboard. The good summer

had bones, like you. Like a moth in the long light.
As did the parsley in its second year. Even before I saw the snow melt

on the street like deer eyes,
I had felt the pureness of joy as unrefrigerated, mixable.

I lay in the garden like a heap of organs,
my hair in boney birdwind, cramping at the heart. I'd dreamt,

and then, my dream dreamt another dream.
I'd felt something, and then, as if my body was improvising

its borders, my feeling had another. I've yet to write the letters;
to everyone who was happy for me.

After the engagement, I'd brush my hair
before bed, use retinol and sunscreen. And some-

times, when you were at work, I'd pull the drawer out, where we kept
the wedding bills and vows. Open the blue box and slip

on my wedding band like I was a chime, knew of wind—
could feel with direction. I want to touch

someone, soon—their eyeball; what ultimate trust.
First you, and then, the plague.

Persephon, Persephone

You are concrete, and it has rained
all afternoon. I am afraid
you will drive to London to lay
inside the manhole by your father's house

and he'll come out and say, *get a grip son!*
while you try to make the water stick
to your childhood
body—you've read somewhere

that clouds absorb
infrared radiation, so you'll hurry
to the graveyard to kneel
into the powdered seed

of your mother's cheeks like the skin
inside a pomegranate. Maybe they'll show
on telly, how you colonise every word
there is for grief. Make podcasts,

titled *Realms of Hades' Husband*.
You will have its rice, its autumnal coal
and creative licence of the word *griefservant*.
I am afraid I'll ask my mother's advice mid-

year of this sadness, and she'll then try
to conserve me. I will tip the ladle
of my hip bones at the bottom
of the food chain, drive north

to feed my pickled
jugular to the seagulls. And so, my mother
will doubt her motherhood
come may: *don't you go out and buy me anything,*

she'd say—and because
I'm a dick, I don't. Some people believe
that the sneeze is the devil's advantage
to enter a human body. How big a gap

must the first cry be—what narcissus
that we cannot resist plucking with our lungs.

You'll come home, slip some ghost-
writer's business card out of your pocket

and tell me, he'd so *love* to write the biography
of your symptoms, before they die
of medication. Tell me, that'd be a yearly
opportunity. We'll both say *touche, touche.*

We'll find that even a death wish comes
with a kidney. That we can harvest
our kingdoms of darkness
and live a little longer.

Small Theories

I've put the cannibal in me aside,
did you notice?—Haven't read you a poem all of August.

When I washed the dishes last night, I saw
my face in the window, and how the broken bulb
was hanging above my head—I thought it suited me.

Even the heart only beats twice-
told to. Keep thinking of the swallows.
The syringe tip, larger than their beaks.

We had the worms and had the water.
We had the opportunity to keep something alive

that wants to be so badly. This is something
I wish to forget—forgetting creates

so much room for the imagination. But that one summer
in California, out with newly found Facebook friends

the older brother of the girl I was with, parked
his car on the bridge, on the side of the highway

to get his denim jacket out of the trunk.
The girl said, he had trouble with short

term memory, and I wanted to shout,
I understand. I'm equally reckless, remembering—

I trust the old memory
more than the life I've built around it.

Seagull Pantoum

after Diane di Prima's 'The Window'

It seems I've known you for the length of music beneath my skin—Lord,
sometimes that is only yesterday. There is bone in my sunlit
body that echoes your smoke. Your blackberry chapeau has browned, but I applaud
your fruit even when you rip yourself from it—

sometimes that is only yesterday's. There is breath beneath sunlit
skin, the aura of a line that laughs through my veins. Do you
know, it claps for your fruit when you rip yourself from it?
The buckled bridge on my feet is only time for the bad years to flow through.

You laugh through my heart, chuckle my blood new.
I can only write the day less knowing than it is, thirstier minutes. Come step
with the buckled bridge of your feet—it's time for the bad years to flow through.
I am afraid, when you don't see yourself, you will drown in the ebb.

I'll write the day younger than it is, seconds in their twenties:
when our love is looking through a shallow window, it is still an eyeful.
I am afraid, when you don't see yourself, you will drown with your berries
and the seagulls, O, the seagulls. Heaven will pick you up like a worm. Guide us

love. To look through a shallow window is still an eyeful.
We've waded through its glass, skipped stones—endured.
O, the seagulls. Heaven would pick you up, a worm. A thing to dine on.
Won't you? It seems I've known him for the length of music beneath my skin, Lord.

The Learned Ascender

To Touch a Rose like an Abacus

His mother, in the living room, but never there,
when I am—I'm only imagining things:

her laughter, her scoliosis.

If no one saw us,
were my hands ever true?

Were his eyes ever jewels, did he ever wear them?

Or, that beaded blouse—did he ever dance
on his mother's tears, the way dust

dances on water, and cannot undo?

Once, I saw his father
did not give

him a doll for christmas

by the way
he touched a rose

like an abacus.

We went out like all people do.
The lamps, shedding their petals—he didn't count.

Didn't try to fix it.

Was he ever a true
mathematician?

My scent, caught

between septum and wing—
I flew in the sky

of his nostrils like my father has told me

a man could make me.
Didn't tell you he's a painter—

didn't say, before

he paints a woman
as steam, he paints

her as a rose—doesn't count, does it.

I mean, sometimes, that's only a mirror.
When he stops, he says, *quit*

your cryin' boy, that's not a man's shirt—lose the silk.

Lays his head
on the door of the bathroom stalls, whistles,

when I long for him, it is always fiction.

My Loneliness as Kafka's Diaries

8 August. The two vases sit on the windowsill, and the slit of dust between them reminds me of a woman's skirt.

After half an hour of reading, loneliness has become academic. I don't interpret anything into its presence—its fact. The knots in my fingers, derived from a precedent love-affair, are a thesis that only proves loneliness is a misshapen thing, that wants everything to look just like it. The only logical conclusion of an argument I have with myself, over which pillow to imagine a lover's head on tonight, is Chimaera. I chase myself around the bed until it is a brothel, meet loneliness in the red room and fall in love with her.

What events can I tell my friends about when we next meet?
The lid would not come off the marmalade jar, the sugar sat on the frontiers and gripped ownership of the land I wanted to screw off, to pass through and claim the chunks of orange fields for my mouth. I took a gunmetal spoon—stained silver at least—under the edge of the lid, or was it under the jaw? Then a shot-like sound. You can make a bullet come out of almost anything. These wars, however small, present themselves to me. I already know how bored they will be of my spoongun story, but I would rather not talk about corruption; the money that flows out of my pockets and under the table of mania, to fool myself with shiny new shoes, that will stay carpet-friendly and heel-scouring.

In my dream, my mother speaks Spanish and the postman delivers the wrong letter. We eat chips together, my cousin makes me a sandwich with chocolate spread and marshmallows. And I don't know what to get from that, other than at first I was lonely and misshapen, then suddenly I was not.

Fruit Basket

I give you this plum.
I give you this peach.

This rain coat and this eye.

Portrait of a Spring as a Parody

From the way his childhood rested in the bowl
of his upper lip like his roller skates
in the garden pond—and spilled
into his mouth, forbade with its umami
taste what sweetness there might have been,
I could tell he did not love
me anymore. I've processed
this all throughout February,
in my writing room. Spring came

like a parody of my writing.
Sometimes, when you hear the words
from a lit mouth, it sounds like sun
on lakeskin, polyester sweat—

what purpose does reality have,
if it can be changed?—Facts
like linen being spun
from my amygdala.

Hourglass

One night, when my body was without
        a title and I underlined want instead,

he said only *hush, hush.*
        I picked him up at a bar, like a cherry

stone out of wet grass. What a bird-
        like thing of me to do, to expect something soft

from someone all backbone.
        He was beside the sand in the hour,

like a fish caressed
        with a rock. And the stars

had so much foam in their mouths—
        mother taught me not to stare;

sometimes I am bitten with wishes
        that could only be male.

There, his moon berries in fox piss,
        there, my mouth's allowance

spent on baskets. There was a man
        at the train station, who hypnotised

the nicotine out of my lungs with the way
        his yellowed fingers dragged the smoke

around his body, like he was cloning himself
        into a version of eternity.

How men can make themselves
        into anything they want to,

a language beside the tongue.
        In bed, I reached for my cigarettes,

filtered his hot sand from lip to lip
        until it was glass and he was running

through himself like memory.
Until he couldn't remember himself.

Kiwi Science

So we're young,
      so we're summer-
                swoon and Jesus-full—
         we're all miracle
    makers: between Dixie
        toilets and up-hill races,
we lay our hands
on the experience of heartbeat
from another chest
and learn to walk. We're all wet
for one boy   and it turns out he likes me—
    I forget I have a bible-
thick moustache and unshaven legs.
    I forget my friend
had eaten a kiwi,
and her tongue bloomed in the
spoon like an early peony.
        We were young enough
to make mistakes just to pray for
a miracle, and despite our youngness
and new-found gospel
of Darwin's theory, in which hungry gods
adapt to their believers for the pure
sake of survival,
I should have been a better friend.
So we're post-lit
backyards and bible study,
car cinemas—after-young,
growing our first greys like sermons
of our thirties, having children.
What old miracle remained among the new
is the holy presence of your friendship.

Enough to Look

When I met my husband, I was in a terrible state.
But, I had my hair extensions. I'd curl
and crimp, wear the messy bun that had always been
too flimsy with my own hair,
and fool myself enough to leave
the clips of strands in, when washing mine—I had him
fooled real good, too; with the towel on my head
my movement was cautious enough to look graceful—I'd braid
and braid the three of us. But, there came a point,
when I couldn't take it anymore.
We'd been wearing ourselves open
on each others' shoulders, not long after
my hair was thin and short, again. I was lying
in bed, and I confessed to him:
"I never went to the hairdresser's!"
There has always been a need for light—either the giving,
or the receiving. Knowledge, gossip, forgiveness.
Eden and Icarus. We ask of the dying, "walk
toward the light!" I've often felt like I've been building
towers of Babylon, instead of writing poems—
I walk from the room of dark, into the room of darkness,
into the room of the next day. To my husband
I say, "it's empty here!" but, I have a gambling fear that's not all
true. Lately, I've been up at four, sitting with the wolves
of TV towers, about two miles out from our porch, their eyes, a milk-
red glare in the night, calling their curious
cubs, warning, "don't come any closer, there is danger."

Love Poem as Oblivion

Somewhen, I'll forget you like a tear on a harpoon. Fumble with the aerodynamics of your name and it will not return to me. The golden wraparound skirt grandma got and gave you glitters, lost in chronology. And it's not how mother wore it, still in Canada, or how I never got to see it. But how we are made of this memory: you tug at the hem of the field like a hornet at the last light. And it's not how every house was her buoy, but how her voice was the first time you bathed without listening to Sia, but to how mother's darjeeling sounded, sat on an e-minor piano, rippled and ruffled as a sepia brain, brown cornflower-wind, already like Wilhelmshaven's shore gunk. Twice today, white monarchs flew from my pelvis. You bring a face and I remember it in olives. We've yet to settle for language, the iris is too big a molecule. You swing into me and the opposite of memory sways, which in this newton's cradle must mean, forgetting is the same as a future. Live here a while, blue like a fox in water. I've grieved you more than any love I've laboured for you. I'd like so much to forget your braid, but not the hands who made it.

What Good

I laugh & wonder   how good.   What good? That, I wanted to tell you.
         The last postcard I got was one of a naked woman
& and it was just when the neighbour was out sweeping
         dead things around in his garden. I was going on the assumption that she'd be closing
her eyes, so that's really the only reason I kissed her. Because once,
         there were maples by sandhills, by a quarry lake, east of town. I was young
of who I am now, & stood near none of it—just May peeking through
         my fingers. It's another draft of the same May. My husband's worn
of the same poem. But he kisses me with open eyes. If you wrote to me, I wouldn't know
         how to answer—lick the stamp with soap. Even my laughter
is a sequence I am playing back into my belly
         on an ill-tuned guitar. Go on, squeeze this hand together, I will be invisible, a window,
                                                                                                  or both.